Animals in Summer

BY MADDIE SPALDING

The Child's World®
childsworld.com

Published by The Child's World®
1980 Lookout Drive • Mankato, MN 56003-1705
800-599-READ • www.childsworld.com

Photographs ©: Olivier Blondeau/iStockphoto, cover,
1; Mark Caunt/Shutterstock Images, 5; iStockphoto,
6–7, 8–9, 10–11, 19; Lucy Wightman/iStockphoto,
12–13; Galyna Andrushk/Shutterstock Images, 14–15;
Sumiko Photo/iStockphoto, 17; Shutterstock Images,
20–21; Red Line Editorial, 22

ISBN 9781503823778
LCCN 2017944897

Printed in the United States of America
PA02358

ABOUT THE AUTHOR

Maddie Spalding is a writer and
editor who lives in Minnesota. She
has written more than 20 books for
children. Her favorite summertime
activity is spending time with family
at their lakeside cabin.

Contents

Keeping Cool

It is summer! A rabbit rests in a **burrow**. Shade keeps the rabbit cool.

A turtle warms itself on a rock. Then it slides into a pond.

Summer is hot.
Animals do not
need as much fur.
They **shed** their fur
to keep cool.

8

Finding Food

Flowers bloom.

Hummingbirds drink **nectar**
from flowers.

Plants grow. Deer eat the plants. They find plenty of food.

Grizzly bears eat fish. They find seeds and berries.

Bees collect nectar from flowers. They bring it back to their **hives**. They turn it into honey.

Changes

Some animals change color. Arctic foxes turn brown in summer. This helps them sneak up on **prey**.

Some hares also turn brown. This helps them hide from **predators**.

Pom-Pom Hummingbird

Make your own pom-pom hummingbird!

Supplies:

1 toothpick	glue
1 muffin cup	black marker
2 large pom-pom balls	scissors
2 wiggly eyes	

Instructions:

1. Use the marker to color the toothpick. Cut the toothpick in half.

2. Glue the pom-pom balls together. Glue eyes onto one ball.

3. Cut the muffin cup into four equal pieces. Glue two pieces on either side of the pom-pom ball. These are the wings.

4. Glue one piece of the muffin cup onto the bottom of the pom-pom ball. This is the tail. Now you have a hummingbird!

Glossary

burrow—(BUR-oh) A burrow is a tunnel or a hole in the ground made or used as a home for animals. A rabbit rests in a burrow to keep cool in summer.

hives—(HIVES) Hives are nests where bees live. Bees bring nectar back to their hives.

nectar—(NEK-tur) Nectar is a sweet liquid in flowers. Hummingbirds drink nectar.

predators—(PRED-uh-turz) Predators hunt other animals for food. Arctic foxes are predators.

prey—(PRAY) Prey are animals that are hunted by other animals for food. Arctic hares are prey.

shed—(SHED) To shed is to let something fall off. Wolves shed some of their fur in summer.

To Learn More

Books

Amoroso, Cynthia. *Summer*. Mankato, MN: The Child's World, 2014.

Pearson, Carrie A. *A Cool Summer Tail*. Mount Pleasant, SC: Sylvan Dell, 2014.

Walters, Jennifer Marino. *Sweet Summer*. Concord, MA: Rocking Chair Kids, 2016.

Web Sites

Visit our Web site for links about summer animals:

childsworld.com/links

Note to Parents, Teachers, and Librarians: We routinely verify our Web links to make sure they are safe and active sites. So encourage your readers to check them out!

Index